LOVE BEYOND LOOKS

A 5-Week Bible Study
On Body Image

KASEY SHULER

To all the women who struggle with body image: you are loved, and so you are beautiful. Hear this good news from a God who loves you:

But now thus says the Lord,
he who created you, O Jacob,
he who formed you, O Israel:
"Fear not, for I have redeemed you;
I have called you by name, you are mine."
ISAIAH 43:1

CONTENTS

Introduction   *v*

Leader Guide   *vii*

WEEK ONE   How Do You See Yourself?   *1*

WEEK TWO   How Does God See You?   *13*

WEEK THREE   How Do You See Others?   *27*

WEEK FOUR   How Do You See God?   *43*

WEEK FIVE   Leaving A Legacy   *57*

Conclusion   *71*

Notes   *72*

About The Author   *73*

INTRODUCTION

Oh, body image. It starts when we first see our face in the mirror. I remember when my daughter could see her face in a mirror that was suspended above her play mat, and she would smile at herself for at least ten minutes. It was the best — I finally had time to clean out the gross smell coming from the fridge without interruptions! It was also delightful to see that sweet three-month-old finding such pure and innocent joy in her own image. However, we all know that changes pretty soon. By the time little girls are ten, only 11% call themselves beautiful.[1]

What happened? Do we stay on that path of discontentment through puberty, adolescence, pregnancy, and motherhood? How can we get back to feeling pure joy when we see our own image, not because of outward beauty, but because it's good that God made us in his image? We can find contentment knowing that a good God makes good creations; more importantly, he looks beyond the outward appearance to the heart.

This five week study is designed for you to work through on your own, and preferably for a group of women, with the purpose of gaining a deeper understanding about what 1 Samuel 16:7b means: "For the Lord sees not as man sees: man looks on the outward appearance, but the Lord looks on the heart." We will explore how you view your own outward appearance, how God sees you, how you see others, how you see God, and finally, how you can leave a legacy of positive body image that lasts beyond your own life.

During this study, I researched several groups of women, and began with a simple question: "What do you see when you look in the mirror?" A few of the participants agreed to share their stories for the study, but I changed their names to protect their privacy. This Bible study is not just my work, it is our work. I share their experiences not only because I think they are beautiful, but because I hope you too can relate to them.

HOW IT WORKS

You can do this study on your own or in a group setting. I recommend that you find at least one other person to do it with so you can discuss, ask questions, find answers, pray with and for each other, and follow-up with one another after the session has ended.

Each week of the study consists of three elements:
1. One memorization scripture per week: Unless otherwise noted, all verses are from the English Standard Version (ESV).
2. Four days of individual sessions with questions and a prayer, or other challenge for the week.
3. One final day of group discussion.

You can certainly do all of the sessions in one day, but the daily sessions give you more time to store scripture in your heart and refresh your mind, allowing you to contemplate new questions each day. Some of the questions require you to dwell on an idea throughout the week, or to serve someone else, so try not to wait until the last minute.

If you read anything that really resonates with your soul, please don't let that moment pass you by. Thank God in prayer for revealing Himself to you, then share it with others! Faith is meant for sharing. Stop and highlight the phrase or verse, then at the end of that day or week, share that with your group in discussion. You can also tag your favorites on social media with #lovebeyondlooks. Let's follow Jesus together and change the conversation around healthy body image. We are small, but our God is great and can do immeasurably more than we can ask or imagine (Ephesians 3:20).

These questions will require introspection and soul searching, but don't let this become a burden. If you can walk away from the study with a greater understanding of who God is and who you are in Christ, consider it a worthy investment of your time and energy.

INSTRUCTIONS

1. Gather a few friends and decide on a day and time to meet each week for five weeks.
2. Work through the study for four days of the week prior to meeting with your group, writing down each week's memory verse and the answers to each question.
3. Meet and discuss the questions from that week.
4. Change our culture's conversation on body image by using the tag #lovedbeyondlooks on social media.
5. For additional tools, go to kaseybshuler.com.

LEADER GUIDE

Characteristics of a Leader

1. Love Jesus
2. Preferably be a member of a local church

Leader Notes

Start each week by praying for each person in your group of women by name, and continue to pray for them throughout the week. Contact each person at least once during the week to check-in with them to see how they are doing.

At the beginning of each week, remind the women in your group that the discussion stays within the walls of the room. However, if someone reveals something about herself that is harmful or harmful to someone else, you are obligated to seek help for that person, such as a pastor or health professional.

You don't need to have all the answers. If you do have an answer based on God's word, great! If there are any lingering unanswered questions after group, make a note to do a little research before next time. Your role is to lead discussion and love each person like Jesus does; the Holy Spirit will provide the right answers.

The study questions are guidelines. The goal is to soak in scriptural truth and speak from the heart. If that means you cover one question during the Group Discussion but have an hour-long conversation about an issue that needs addressing, go for that. If you don't feel like that conversation is appropriate for the Group Discussion, make a point to lovingly say that you will talk with that person outside of group, so you can hear from others. Let the Spirit lead!

If there are more than twelve people in the group, split up the core group into smaller groups of three or four for the discussion, and appoint a leader for each small group. The study discussion questions work best in a small group setting.

During Group Discussion, don't feel like everyone has to answer every single question. If you are going through the past week's lesson, and nobody has an answer, you can give your own and wait to see if that encourages anyone to share her answer, or just move on to the next question.

Be intentional about starting and ending at an agreed-upon time in order to respect everyone's time.

HOW DO YOU SEE YOURSELF?

DAY ONE

How Do You See Yourself?

I praise you because I am fearfully and wonderfully made. Wonderful are

your works; my soul knows it very well.

PSALM 139:14

MYSTERIOUSLY, GOD CREATED a visible creation out of invisible things. Don't even try wrapping your head around that one. One-hundred years from now, you will be in your thinking chair, covered in cobwebs, pondering this question. What we do know is that the Bible tells us in Psalm 139 that God very carefully crafted us in our mother's womb. He took time to create every perfect detail about us! He is God, and even though we don't always understand him, he surely doesn't create mistakes. God created beauty itself, and since we are made in his image, then we are also beautiful and wonderful. In order to be satisfied with our own appearance, we must be satisfied and trust in the God who made us (John 14:1).

Praying scripture, which is God-breathed, is powerful (2 Timothy 3:16). Start each session by ***praying***, that unlike the Israelites, who wandered in the desert for 40 years, the Holy Spirit will give you eyes to see, ears to hear, and a heart to understand God's word today (Deuteronomy 29:4). Then, **write down** the memory verse of the week from above (Psalm 139:14):

I praise you because I am fearfully + wonderfully made. Wonderful are your works; my soul Knows it very well.

Talk It Out

1. "When I look in the mirror, I don't think about it too much, but when I do feel bad about myself it affects my day and my relationships. How I feel about my body can either empower me or hinder me." –Lori

   Look in the mirror. What do you see and why?
   A.   Ugh, I'd rather not look in the mirror
   B.   Just okay, but I could change a few things
   C.   Hello, beautiful!
   D.   None of the above

2. Imagine you're at the foot of a majestic mountain. How do you feel? Now imagine you're at the top of that mountain. Combine those two feelings, and that's how a positive body image can be. You're the crown of creation standing in the midst of an awe-inspiring

Creator, and you feel simultaneously confident and humbled. What does this balance of body image look like for you?

3. Think about how much time and energy you put into your body—the time it takes to try to feel and look good. Is it worth it for you? If not, how could you spend less time and energy, and where would you redirect that time?

Take It With You

God gave us a body to look a certain way, just as he gave us certain abilities. He purposefully made every single detail about you for his greater glory, and wants you to capture the joy that comes from walking in his plans. *Meditate* on this week's memory verse: Psalm 139:14. *Think* about what this verse means to you each time you look in the mirror. *Write down* Psalm 139:14 and tape it to your bathroom mirror. May it be a reminder of how God sees you every time you see yourself in the mirror.

Day Two

Where Did You Get This Picture of Yourself?

Pray for eyes to see, ears to hear, and a heart to understand God's word today (Deuteronomy 29:4). **Write down** Psalm 139:14, or say it out loud.

I praise you because I am fearfully + wonderfully made; Wonderful are your works; my soul Knows it Very well.

One of the best ways we can discover our present is to look to our past. Louisa shares her story of her mom's influence on her childhood and how she wants to influence her future children:

As a young adult, I struggle with feeling like I'm 'failing' with my health and fitness if I am not pursuing a new diet, goal, plan or philosophy. Looking back on my childhood, it has become clear that part of the reason I struggle with this is because it was modeled to me by my mom. My mom is a wonderful, God-fearing woman, but she has always struggled with body image. As long as I can remember, she was always pursuing some sort of diet: South Beach, Weight Watchers, Atkins, Carb Lovers, and never spoke with contentedness about her body. She was never pleased with it and only saw how it could be improved.

I hope that my mom and I can learn to take to heart the redeeming work and artistry of our Creator, and find rest in that—a respite from the daily grind of a diet's ridiculing law—so that I can model something different for my children someday.

Talk It Out

1. What kind of health habits did your family have growing up?

2. How have your peers impacted your attitudes and actions about appearance throughout your life? Can you think of any specific examples?

3. How has media and culture affected how you see your own body?

Take It With You

Read Proverbs 31:30: "Charm is deceitful, and beauty is vain, but a woman who fears the Lord is to be praised." Beauty is certainly good, but sometimes we can put too much emphasis on outward beauty. The world may praise women for their beauty and charm, but fear of the Lord is even more important and lasting. *Ask* the Lord to place a greater desire for him in your heart than the desire to look good.

Day Three

How Does This Picture Affect Your Heart?

Pray for eyes to see, ears to hear, and a heart to understand God's word today (Deuteronomy 29:4). Then, **write down** Psalm 139:14 or say it out loud:

When I don't feel good about my body, I don't feel good about life. I feel like I'm wearing negative Nancy glasses. I'm hesitant to go out and meet new people, I don't want my husband to touch me, and I cringe when I look in the mirror. And the strange part is, I might look exactly the same as yesterday when I felt good about myself.

The only difference is the posture of my heart. When I'm not grateful about the gift of my body, I'm grumbling about life in general. When my heart is feeling grateful about my body, I'm feeling grateful about life. I have less time to worry about me and more emotional energy to serve others. I'm more confident. I'm nicer to my husband. I can focus on the needs of others instead of navel-gazing (it still pokes out from pregnancy, so it's kind of hard to miss). I look in the mirror and am content.

Talk It Out

1. Do you ever have days where you feel better or worse about your body image?

Why?

2. How does the state of your heart affect your actions and relationships?

Take It With You

Think about 1 John 3:20 which says, "whenever our hearts condemn us, God is bigger than our hearts." **Ask** God to renew your mind and heart to view yourself as he does, the same God who created you after the likeness of himself. **Read** over Romans 12:2, and **pray** these verses over your own life.

DAY FOUR

How Can You Get A Right Heart?

Pray for eyes to see, ears to hear, and a heart to understand God's word today (Deuteronomy 29:4). Then, **write down** Psalm 139:14 or say it out loud.

Have you ever made something that you were really proud of? My sister and I took pottery class when we were little, and my sweet mom kept our precious creations over the years, bless her soul. They are absolutely hideous—uneven, misshapen, and almost unrecognizable lumps of baked clay. It's safe to say that God definitely one-upped me on the pottery front.

Think of how God feels about making living creatures out of the dust from the ground and from a single bone. If you can't imagine how much love he feels about his creations, think about the endless, selfless love you have for your parents, your spouse, your children, or other family and friends.

Read Genesis 2. Now, focus on the following:

> ...then the Lord God formed the man of dust from the ground and breathed into his nostrils the breath of life, and the man became a living creature. GENESIS 2:7

> So the Lord God caused a deep sleep to fall upon the man, and while he slept took one of his ribs and closed up its place with flesh. And the rib that the Lord God had taken from the man he made into a woman and brought her to the man. GENESIS 2:21-22

Talk It Out

1. God made both man and woman in his image and declared them good (Genesis 1:31). Has there been a time that you have disagreed with God on this?

2. When we reflect God, we glow with his light, like Moses in Exodus 34:29. We reflect God most when we spend time with him. Others will notice and get a glimpse of his beauty through you. Are you more concerned with your own image than reflecting God?

Take It With You

Think about how excited God must have been to make man and woman, the crown of his creation, and to see the joy in his eyes as he brought the two together. Imagine the scenario. Do you think they posted selfies together and obsessed over their wedding day preparations?

They saw each other and the man rejoiced in song (Genesis 2:23)! Adam rejoiced because what he saw was beautiful. Because what God made was beautiful. Because God made woman after his own image, we need to be more concerned with how we are reflecting God than with our own image.

According to Proverbs 4:23, right priorities start with the heart, and work their way out. Keep your heart with all vigilance! For from it flow the springs of life. I don't need to convince you that you're beautiful. I want you to believe that God is beautiful, he made you, he knows you fully, loves you completely, and is with you always. And just for the record, he thinks you are beautiful whether you agree with him or not.

Focus on how much God loves you and how wonderful he thinks you are, not because you're awesome but because you're his. When you believe this truth with all your heart, your heart will not only be full, but will overflow with the abundance of joy in Christ.

Group Discussion

Catch up with one another. Drink good drinks, eat good food, go for a drive, or go on a walk together.

1. Pray for God's name to be made holy, for humble hearts, and for honest conversation.
2. Recite Psalm 139:14 out loud to someone or recite it together as a group.
3. Review your answers from this past week.
4. Concluding questions:

    a. How has your view of your outward appearance changed since the beginning of this week?
    b. How can you maintain a God-centered focus of your outward appearance?

5. Conclude in prayer. Start by reading this verse out loud: "Whoever finds his life will lose it, and whoever loses his life for my sake will find it" (Matthew 10:39). Then, give thanks to God in prayer for making you fearfully and wonderfully. Ask the Holy Spirit to help you see yourself the way he does, and to place your focus on the image of Jesus.

WEEK TWO

HOW DOES GOD SEE YOU?

DAY ONE

How Does God See Your Outward Appearance?

Do not look on his appearance or on the height of his stature, because I have rejected him. For the Lord sees not as man sees: man looks on the outward appearance, but the Lord looks on the heart.

1 SAMUEL 16:7

PRAY FOR EYES TO SEE, ears to hear, and a heart to understand God's word today (Deuteronomy 29:4). Then, **write down** the memory verse of the week or say it out loud:

Read the story of Samuel anointing David as king in 1 Samuel 16:1-13. Samuel was sure that the Lord had anointed David's brother Eliab because he was tall and good-looking—because powerful people are tall and good-looking, right? But the Lord spoke to Samuel in verse 7 and said, "Do not look on his appearance or on the height of his stature, because I have rejected him. For the Lord sees not as man sees: man looks on the outward appearance, but the Lord looks on the heart."

Even Samuel, who was a righteous man of God, looked at Eliab's appearance before he saw the contents of his heart.

Talk It Out

1. What do you think the Lord sees when he looks at you?

2. Think about last week's lesson and what you see when you look in the mirror. Have you ever complained about your body? To whom are you directing your complaints? See God's response in Romans 9:20. You are unique for a reason! It's okay to want to change things about your body, but it's not okay to complain about them. God designed us to be a certain way, and then there are certain things we have done to our bodies over time, like overeating, under-exercising, and over-stressing.

    We can to learn how to embrace the features God has given us and submit ourselves, including our bodies, to the Spirit of self-control (Galatians 5:16, Galatians 5:22, 1 Corinthians 9:27, 2 Timothy 1:7). Pray for that self-control in your daily life and remember that God has not given us any temptation we cannot handle (1 Corinthians 10:13). Learn how to embrace your features by writing down three things about your body for which you are grateful (example: I'm grateful for my strong legs, my green eyes, my skin complexion). Do this each time you look in the mirror.

1.

2.

3.

3. Ephesians 1:4 (New Living Translation) says that, "Even before he made the world, God loved us and chose us in Christ to be holy and without fault in His eyes." How is this possible? Do you believe you are without fault in his eyes? Why or why not?

Take It With You

If I put on a cap and gown, would people call me a graduate? If I wear a white coat, am I a doctor? We put on clothes that represent who we are. Galatians 3:27 says that when we are baptized in Christ, we put on Christ. We put on his righteousness and holiness (2 Corinthians 5:21).

Just as the Israelites covered their doors with the blood of the lamb during the Passover (Exodus 12), we cover ourselves with the blood of the lamb of God. We aren't just covered on the outside with Christ's righteousness—God gives our hearts the Holy Spirit to gradually renew us from the inside out when we let him (Ephesians 4:22-24). Every time you get dressed for the day, think of how you put on Christ's righteousness, and take time to *give thanks* that God sees perfection in you from Jesus. **Ask** the Lord for humility to let the Spirit do the work of renewal in you from the inside out.

Day Two

Where Did You Get That Picture?

Pray for eyes to see, ears to hear, and a heart to understand God's word today (Deuteronomy 29:4). Then, **write down** 1 Samuel 16:7 or say it out loud.

It can be challenging to determine where we get our preconceived notions of body image. Let's dig deep and look back to the story of Adam and Eve, the first man and woman to deal with body image issues:

So when the woman saw that the tree was good for food, and that it was a delight to the eyes, and that the tree was to be desired to make one wise, she took of its fruit and ate, and she also gave some to her husband who was with her, and he ate. Then the eyes of both were opened, and they knew that they were naked. And they sewed fig leaves together and made themselves loincloths.

And they heard the sound of the LORD God walking in the garden in the cool of the day, and the man and his wife hid themselves from the presence of the LORD God among the trees of the garden. But the LORD God called to the man and said to him, 'Where are you?' And he said, 'I heard the sound of you in the garden, and I was afraid, because I was naked, and I hid myself.' He said, 'Who told you that you were naked? Have you eaten of the tree of which I commanded you not to eat?' GENESIS 3:6-11

Talk It Out

1. Adam and Eve trusted the words of an evil snake over the words of their good Creator. What happened when they did this? As soon as they believed those lies, they looked at their bodies and felt ashamed—and they had perfect bodies. Body shame is the direct result of believing lies about yourself. What do you think God thought about Adam and Eve at this point?

2. Why did Adam and Eve feel like they needed to hide from God? See Psalm 139:7, 1 Samuel 6:20 for examples from scripture.

3. What lies has the Enemy been whispering to you? What are you doing with those lies?

    Bring lies to the light and they become light (Ephesians 5:13-14). Bring lies to your soul and they become shame. In one column, write down comments others have made about your outward appearance, or ideas you have about your own body. In the other column, write down if you think that thought is a lie or a truth. If you think of any, write down scripture references alongside them. Don't be afraid to write down something positive that is truthful. Writing down positive things about yourself is not prideful when we attribute them to the work of God.

Example:

What I've Heard About Myself	Truth Or Lie	Scripture
I should wear more makeup	Lie	1 Peter 3:3-4
I have a nice smile	Truth	Proverbs 15:13
I have good skin complexion	Truth	Psalm 34:5

Your Turn:

What I've Heard About Myself	Truth Or Lie	Scripture

Take It With You

Did you write down any scripture truths to combat the above lies? Make a point to **memorize** those scriptures so you can use them when you begin to hear lies (Psalm 119:11, Matthew 4:1-11, Ephesians 6:17).

How Does God See Your Heart?

Pray for eyes to see, ears to hear, and a heart to understand God's word today (Deuteronomy 29:4). *Write down* 1 Samuel 16:7 or say it out loud.

We have touched on the subject of how God sees us on the outside, but what does he think about our hearts? Take a look at the passage from Ezekiel below and answer the questions for some insight:

> And I will give them one heart, and a new spirit I will put within them. I will remove the heart of stone from their flesh and give them a heart of flesh, that they may walk in my statutes and keep my rules and obey them. And they shall be my people, and I will be their God. But as for those whose heart goes after their detestable things and their abominations, I will bring their deeds upon their own heads, declares the Lord GOD. Ezekiel 11:19-21

Talk It Out

1. Think about the two hearts God mentions in the above passage. A heart of flesh is a soft, responsive, moldable heart. A heart of stone is a petrified heart, one that is so frightened it is unable to move. It has been turned into a stony, static substance.

Which kind of heart do you have and why?

2. Did God repair the heart of stone? What did he do? Has he healed you from a heart of stone?

3. What happens to those he gives hearts of flesh? What about those whose hearts run after other things? Is this fair? Why or why not? For some biblical perspective, see Exodus 34:6-7.

Take It With You

Give thanks to God that he has given you a new heart, and **pray** for the obedience to respond to him when he calls. *Know* that you can trust him, because he gave you a new heart, new desires, and a new purpose. He puts his own Spirit in us, and he will be faithful even when we are not.

DAY FOUR

How Can You Get A Right Heart?

Pray for eyes to see, ears to hear, and a heart to understand God's word today (Deuteronomy 29:4). Then, **write down** 1 Samuel 16:7 or say it out loud.

You are the crowning jewel of God's creation. He saved the best for last. You were made in his very image, and you have unimaginable value. You may be working a minimum wage job and have $5 to your name, but you have more value than all the world could offer. You are the daughter of the true King. Don't believe me?

Read the following verses to remind you of this truth. All the verses below are from the English Standard Version:

...even as he chose us in him before the foundation of the world, that we should be holy and blameless before him. In love he predestined us for adoption as sons through Jesus Christ, according to the purpose of his will... EPHESIANS 1:4-5

For we are his workmanship, created in Christ Jesus for good works, which God prepared beforehand, that we should walk in them. EPHESIANS 2:10

So then you are no longer strangers and aliens, but you are fellow citizens with the saints and members of the household of God. EPHESIANS 2:19

And you, who were dead in your trespasses and the uncircumcision of your flesh, God made alive together with him, having forgiven us all our trespasses, by canceling the record of debt that stood against us with its legal demands. This he set aside, nailing it to the cross. COLOSSIANS 2:13-14

For you have died, and your life is hidden with Christ in God. When Christ who is your life appears, then you also will appear with him in glory. COLOSSIANS 3:3-4

And because you are sons, God has sent the Spirit of his Son into our hearts, crying, "Abba! Father!" So you are no longer a slave, but a son, and if a son, then an heir through God. GALATIANS 4:6-7

...for in Christ Jesus you are all sons of God, through faith. For as many of you as were baptized into Christ have put on Christ. GALATIANS 3:26-27

Do you not know that you are God's temple and that God's Spirit dwells in you? 1 CORINTHIANS 3:16

Therefore, if anyone is in Christ, he is a new creation. The old has passed away; behold, the new has come. All this is from God, who through Christ reconciled us to himself and gave us the ministry of reconciliation; that is, in Christ God was reconciling the world to, not counting their trespasses against them, and entrusting to us the message of reconciliation. Therefore, we are ambassadors for Christ, God making his appeal through us. We implore you on behalf of Christ, be reconciled to God. For our sake he made him to be sin who knew no sin, so that in him we might become the righteousness of God. 2 CORINTHIANS 5:17-21

But you are a chosen race, a royal priesthood, a holy nation, a people for his own possession, that you may proclaim the excellencies of him who called you out of darkness into his marvelous light. 1 PETER 2:9

Talk It Out

Can you think of any other verses that speak to you about your identity? As you read the Bible, note the verses that speak to you about how God sees you by enclosing them in parentheses. Remember, these verses are a symbol and a reminder that God surrounds you while forming you into the image of Christ.

Take It With You

Write down the verse that speaks to you. **Place it** somewhere that you will see it daily as a reminder of God's uncompromising love for you.

Group Discussion

Catch up with one another. Drink good drinks, eat good food, go for a drive, or go on a walk together.

1. Pray for God's name to be made holy, for humble hearts, and for honest conversation.
2. Recite 1 Samuel 16:7 out loud to someone or recite it as a group.

3. Review your answers from this past week's session.

4. Concluding questions:

    a. What from this week stood out about how God sees you?

    b. Do you have any doubts about how God views us in 1 Samuel 16:7?

5. Conclude in prayer. Start by reading this verse out loud: "So she called the name of the LORD who spoke to her, 'You are [El-Roi,] a God of seeing,' for she said, 'Truly here I have seen him who looks after me'" (Genesis 16:13). Then, pray that God would renew your mind and open your eyes to see the marvelous truth that God views you as a perfect creation,. Ask the Holy Spirit for faith to remember God's love for you in Christ.

WEEK THREE

HOW DO YOU SEE OTHERS?

How Do You See Others?

A new commandment I give to you, that you love one another: just as I

have loved you, you also are to love one another.

JOHN 13:34

PRAY FOR EYES TO SEE, ears to hear, and a heart to understand God's word today (Deuteronomy 29:4). Then, **write down** the memory verse of the week or say it out loud:

The way you view yourself, and how God views you, has a direct affect on others and how they learn to view themselves. You love people when you see them for who they are, as image-bearers of our Creator.

How do you see the people around you? Do you look at them and see their outward appearance, or do you see them for who they are and the innate value they carry as human beings with eternal souls? Unfortunately, there can be a difference in the grace we extend to people we are acquainted with and those we aren't. For those we don't personally know, we fall back on physical appearance, which is the easiest way to form an opinion (but not the most accurate). Once we do get to know that person, we are able to look beyond their exterior and love them for who they are.

Talk It Out

1. Even the Bible mentions people's appearances. 1 Samuel 16:1-3 says that man looks at the appearance, and it's true. Let's take a look at a few practical examples from the Bible regarding a superficial awareness of people compared to a deeper understanding of who they really are.

Superficial Knowledge

a. *Cultural standards:*

Judge for yourselves: is it proper for a wife to pray to God with her head uncovered? Does not nature itself teach you that if a man wears long hair it is a disgrace for him, but if a woman has long hair, it is her glory? For her hair is given to her for a covering. 1 CORINTHIANS 11:13-15

b. *Disdain:*

And when the Philistine looked and saw David, he disdained him, for he was but a youth, ruddy and handsome in appearance. 1 SAMUEL 17:42

c. *Leadership potential:*

And he had a son whose name was Saul, a handsome young man. There was not a man among the people of Israel more handsome than he. From his shoulders upward he was taller than any of the people. 1 SAMUEL 9:2

d. *Physical attraction:*

Now Laban had two daughters. The name of the older was Leah, and the name of the younger was Rachel. Leah's eyes were weak, but Rachel was beautiful in form and appearance. Jacob loved Rachel. And he said, 'I will serve you seven years for your younger daughter Rachel.' GENESIS 29:16-18

e. *Simple description:*

And he was seeking to see who Jesus was, but on account of the crowd he could not, because he was small in stature. LUKE 19:3

Deeper Knowledge

a. *Romantic relationship:*

Behold, you are beautiful, my love, behold, you are beautiful! Your eyes are doves behind your veil. Your hair is like a flock of goats leaping down the slopes of Gilead. Your teeth are like a flock of shorn ewes that have come up from the washing, all of which bear twins, and not one among them has lost its young. SONG OF SOLOMON 4:1-2

b. *Creator and creation:*

> ...and in the midst of the lampstands one like a son of man, clothed with a long robe and with a golden sash around his chest. The hairs of his head were white, like white wool, like snow. His eyes were like a flame of fire, his feet were like burnished bronze, refined in a furnace, and his voice was like the roar of many waters. In his right hand he held seven stars, from his mouth came a sharp two-edged sword, and his face was like the sun shining in full strength.
> REVELATION 1:13-16

Write down the similarities and differences in how the Bible speaks about superficial appearances of some people in comparison with a deeper knowledge of others.

2. Think about someone you saw today but don't know on a personal level. Write down their name and your perception of them.

   Now think of someone that you know personally. Write down their name and your perception of them.

3. How do your answers compare for the two people mentioned above?

Take It With You

After we get to know someone, first impressions based on outward appearance become second tier to the person's inward character. One thing that stands in these verses is the level of detail in physical descriptions of people the author knows. Those physical descriptions go way beyond hair color and body build. The author displays a deeper love by how they describe their loved one—a love beyond looks that makes the other person even more attractive.

The more we love someone, the more beautiful they become. Solomon, in Song of Solomon, even goes so far as to tell his love that there is no flaw in her (Song of Solomon 4:7). In Revelation 1:13-16 above, Jesus reveals His true appearance to John, who he knew and deeply loved. John was then willing to share that description with all of us through God's Word, because God knows and loves us.

Revisit last week's lesson to get a refresher on how God sees us. When we know how God sees us, we can see others as God created them to be. Throughout your day, **keep John 13:34 on your mind and in your heart** when you see people you don't know yet and people you do know. Love others as you have been loved.

DAY TWO

Where Did You Get This Picture of Others?

Pray for eyes to see, ears to hear, and a heart to understand God's word today (Deuteronomy 29:4). Then, **write down** John 13:34, or say it out loud.

We build our ideal view of other people from images and ideologies all around us. Below are examples of stereotypical comments of our culture that can influence our perception of others.

The Culture: "Do it for the thigh gap." Fitspiration
The City: "We're better than you, and we know it!" Globo Gym in *Dodgeball*
The Neighborhood: "Have you seen Ethel's nose ring? She will never get a job looking like a convict!"
The Family: "You can't date him. Birds of a feather flock together."
Personal Experience: "That pretty popular girl is way above my friend league. She would hang out with me if she had nothing better to do, and then dump me when something or someone better comes up."

Satan's goal is to divide and destroy (John 10:10): he tempted Adam and Eve to sin, which divided them and the rest of humanity from God. Since then, he has been trying to divide us through lifestyle choices—ways to eat, work out, dress, date, and even worship. In contrast, the only reason God divides is to further unite us: he divided the curtain that separated us from himself (Ephesians 2:14), and separates our sins from us as far as the east is from the west (Psalm 103:12).

When we look at people and judge them according to their appearance, we are dividing ourselves from them. When we look at loved ones and judge them according to their past or ours, we are dividing ourselves from them and from God.

Talk It Out

1. Picture someone in jail. Now picture someone on the side of the street asking for help. What does each person look like? Do you see

each person as an actual person or a problem? Where did you get that picture (see above examples)?

In this situation, Satan can use race and differing socioeconomic backgrounds to divide us. Read Proverbs 22:2, Proverbs 29:13, Acts 10:34-35, Colossians 3:11, and James 2:9. Write down the verse that speaks to you. What about that verse stands out to you?

2. Think of someone successful in your industry, workplace, school, or realm of influence. What is your perception of them? Where did you get that idea (see above examples)?

The Enemy likes to use jealousy and envy to divide us from our peers (James 3:14-16). Ask the Spirit to search your heart (Psalm 139:23) for any kind of jealousy associated with the person from question two. If you have any of these feelings, write them down, and then ask for the strength to count them better than yourself (Philippians 2:3), and to rejoice when they rejoice (Romans 12:15).

3. Now think of one of your close friends, a family member, or somebody with whom you have a relationship.

Describe them below, and then write down why you described them the way you did.

Did you describe more of their physical features or characteristics? Read 1 Corinthians 13. Did this passage mention appearance? Write down verses from 1 Corinthians 13 that point out ways you can love this person better.

Take It With You

Loving people beyond their looks, beyond their character, and beyond our own cultural and personal assumptions is not easy—in fact, it's impossible for us to do it on our own. It's only when we remember that God first loved us that we can gain the strength to love others.

Read John 13:34 again: "A new commandment I give to you, that you love one another: just as I have loved you, you also are to love one another." **Pray** for each person you mentioned above, and for the Holy Spirit to remind you of God's "Never Stopping, Never Giving up, Unbreaking, Always and Forever Love."[2]

How Do You Value Others Beyond Physical Appearance?

Pray for eyes to see, ears to hear, and a heart to understand God's word today (Deuteronomy 29:4). Then, ***write down*** John 13:34, or say it aloud.

We can compare ourselves with one another, or we can connect with one another. Comparing divides us, and connecting unites us. We need each other too much to constantly compare ourselves with one another. It sounds great on paper, but this is much easier said than done.. Tim Keller, author and pastor, shows us what this would look like in real life:

Wouldn't you like to be the skater who wins the silver, and yet is thrilled about those three triple jumps that the gold medal winner did? To love it the way you love a sunrise? Just to love the fact that it was done? For it not to matter whether it was their success or your success. Not to care if they did it or you did it. You are as happy that they did it as if you had done it yourself—because you are just so happy to see it.[3]

Talk It Out

1. Wouldn't it be wonderful to no longer judge other people by their appearances (John 7:24), be envious of their accomplishments (1 Peter 2:1), or look down on them as failures or for being inexperienced (1 Timothy 4:12), but to love them as we love ourselves? How could we change the world by loving the great

things people do, while giving glory to God for creating such wonderful people around us? Why is it so hard to celebrate others?

2. God tells us to love others as Jesus has loved us. How has Jesus loved you? How can you love and value others beyond their physical appearance?

3. John 7:24 says we should not judge by appearances. Even the world says not to judge a book by its cover. In what ways can we look past physical appearance and see each person as having innate value? Read Genesis 1:27 and Luke 10:25-37 for some biblical perspective on our value as human beings and how we can live that out in our everyday lives.

4. Marriage is the ultimate display of valuing another person. Paul talks about loving the spouse as we love our own body: "In the same way husbands should love their wives as their own bodies. He who loves his wife loves himself. For no one ever hated his own flesh, but nourishes and cherishes it, just as Christ does the church, because we are members of his body" (Ephesians 5:28-30). When a married couple gets old or their physical appearance changes in another way, how do you think their love for each other will change?

5.   We are all born into a family. How do you value your own family members? Do you treat them according to their looks? Why or why not?

Take It With You

All the believers are of one family (John 1:12), and one body: "So we, though many, are one body in Christ, and individually members one of another." If we are one body, we share everything, including celebrations and sorrows: "If one member suffers, all suffer together; if one member is honored, all rejoice together" (1 Corinthians 12:26). **Pray** that God would give you the strength and wisdom to love others as he has loved you, because we are family and are all made in the image of God.

DAY FOUR

How Can You Treat Others With Value?

Pray for eyes to see, ears to hear, and a heart to understand God's word today (Deuteronomy 29:4). Then, *write down* John 13:34 or say it aloud.

Talk It Out

1. We want to love and value others as Jesus has loved us. How has he loved you specifically, and how can you share that with others?

2. One of the most powerful things we can do for others is not just look at them, but see them. To be seen is to be known, and to be known is to be loved. Read Ruth 2:8-13 for an example of how to love across cultural lines, and Genesis 16:1-13 for an example of how to love across socioeconomic lines—both are issues we still face today. How did the women in the story feel loved? What were the risks and rewards of loving these women?

3. Loving others is not always about what you say to them. Loving can also be what you don't say to them. If our intention is to help others by giving them good advice, but it doesn't encourage their faith, it might be more hurtful than helpful. There are so many differing beliefs about everyday things, like eating and drinking (hello, Paleo diet vs. veganism), but these differences do not have to divide us. Paul addresses this in Romans 14:22, saying, "so whatever you believe about these things keep between yourself and God. Blessed is the one who does not condemn himself by what he approves."

    As a general guideline for living with others, Paul encourages us to "pursue what makes for peace and for mutual upbuilding" (Romans 14:19). If you want more specifics, go back and read through Romans 14. Can you think of a time in your life when you realized it was more loving not to speak?

Take It With You

Proverbs 6:24 says "Gracious words are like a honeycomb, sweetness to the soul and health to the body." Challenge yourself to *give* someone the gift of gracious words today; it will make them healthier in body and soul! Write down who you can encourage and how.

John says that we should love in "deed and truth" (1 John 3:18). Write down one tangible thing you can do this week for someone else.

Group Discussion

Catch up with one another. Drink good drinks, eat good food, go for a drive, or go on a walk together.

1. Pray for God's name to be made holy, for humble hearts, and for honest conversation.
2. Recite John 13:35 out loud to someone or recite it as a group.

3. Review your answers from this past week's lesson, then have each person say one thing they like about the people in the room.

4. Concluding questions:

    a. Did you learn anything new about how God wants you to see others?

    b. In what specific ways can you love others this week?

    c. When you said something you liked about each person, did you talk more about what they looked like or their heart?

5. Conclude in prayer. Start by reading this verse aloud: "But if we walk in the light, as he is in the light, we have fellowship with one another, and the blood of Jesus his Son cleanses us from all sin." (1 John 1:7) Then, pray that God would renew your mind in order to change how you see and love others. Ask the Holy Spirit for faith to remember God's love for you in Christ.

WEEK FOUR

HOW DO YOU SEE GOD?

Day One

What Does God Look Like?

And the Word became flesh and dwelt among us, and we have seen his

glory, glory as of the only Son from the Father, full of grace and truth.

John 1:14

Pray for eyes to see, ears to hear, and a heart to understand God's word today (Deuteronomy 29:4). Then, **write down** the memory verse of the week or say it out loud:

We all want to know who we are. We *need* to know who we are. We go to yoga studios and look within ourselves, we create science fiction about our true origins, we look in the mirror in our own bedrooms. How is it that even when we become adults, we still don't know who we are after years of life experience?

We don't know who we are because we are looking to ourselves for the answers instead of our Creator. The apostle Paul addressed our need for soul-searching over 2000 years ago in Acts 17:27-28: "That they should seek God, and perhaps feel their way toward him and find him. Yet he is actually not far from each one of us, for 'In him we live and move and have our being'; as even some of your own poets have said, 'For we are indeed his offspring.'"

God is not just in outer space, and he is not only near, but he is near enough to know him. He wrote 66 books of the Bible so we can get to know him. He sent his Holy Spirit through his Son, Jesus Christ, so we can know him. We don't know ourselves because we don't know God. Let's spend this week reflecting on who God is so we can get to know ourselves too.

Talk It Out

1. Close your eyes and think about what God looks like, and write it down here.

2. In Exodus 33:20, God tells us, "You cannot see my face, for no one may see me and live." However, he does reveal himself in other ways. See Genesis 32:22-30, Exodus 3:6, Exodus 24:17, Numbers 14:14, and 1 Kings 19:11-12 for examples. Write down the verse that stands out to you.

3. God the Father sent Jesus the Son into the world, and miraculously, we saw God as a person. According to the Bible, we can look at Jesus and see the Father, because Jesus represents God's glory exactly:

> And the Word became flesh and dwelt among us, and we have seen his glory, glory as of the only Son from the Father, full of grace and truth. JOHN 1:14

> He is the image of the invisible God, the firstborn of all creation. COLOSSIANS 1:15

> He is the radiance of the glory of God and the exact imprint of his nature. HEBREWS 1:3

If you lived in Jesus' time, would you recognize Jesus as God? Why or why not?

Take It With You

Jesus says, "No one has ever seen God; the only God, who is at the Father's side, he has made him known" (John 1:18). In the Sermon on the Mount, Jesus tells us, "Blessed are the pure in heart, for they will see God" (Matthew 5:8). **Ask** God for a desire to have a pure heart and to see him as he is. He might reveal himself to you in unexpected ways!

Day Two

Where Did You Get That Picture?

Pray for eyes to see, ears to hear, and a heart to understand God's word today (Deuteronomy 29:4). Then, **write down** John 1:14 or say it out loud.

We can get our pictures of God from many places: people in our lives, places, or events in our lives. We may not even realize how we see God or what formed that picture of him until we start searching and asking ourselves the right questions.

Talk It Out

1. Where did you get your picture of God? Did you get it from culture around you? From how other people have treated you? From personal experience? The words of the Bible? Write down anything you think might have influenced your picture of what God looks like.

2. What does your picture of God say about who he is?

3. God is three persons in one, a Trinitarian God (Deuteronomy 6:4). He is Father, Son, and Holy Spirit. Here are some ways the Bible describes the physical appearance of each person:

Father:

> Then Moses and Aaron, Nadab, and Abihu, and seventy of the elders of Israel went up, and they saw the God of Israel. There was under his feet as it were a pavement of sapphire stone, like the very heaven for clearness. And he did not lay his hand on the chief men of the people of Israel; they beheld God, and ate and drank. EXODUS 24:9-11

Son:

> And above the expanse over their heads there was the likeness of a throne, in appearance like sapphire; and seated above the likeness of a throne was a likeness with a human appearance. And upward from what had the appearance of his waist I saw as it were gleaming metal, like the appearance of fire enclosed all around. And downward from what had the appearance of his waist I saw as it were the appearance of fire, and there was brightness around him. Like the appearance of the bow that is in the cloud on the day of rain, so was the appearance of the brightness all around. EZEKIEL 1:26-28

Holy Spirit:

> Now when all the people were baptized, and when Jesus also had been baptized and was praying, the heavens were opened, and the Holy Spirit descended on him in bodily form, like a dove; and a voice came from heaven, "You are my beloved Son; with you I am well pleased." LUKE 3:21-22

What do each of these scriptures say about who God is?

4. Author A.W. Tozer said, "We tend by a secret law of the soul to move toward our mental image of God."[4] What does your mental image of God say about what your soul moves towards?

Take It With You

We tend to focus on physical characteristics, which doesn't line up with the example set by God. Even though God reveals himself in the material world he created, he encourages us in his Word to see his character as more important than his form. God's invisible attributes are too powerful for our mortal eyes and minds to comprehend, and yet, he reveals his character through his creation:

> For his invisible attributes, namely, his eternal power and divine nature, have been clearly perceived, ever since the creation of the world, in the things that have been made. So they are without excuse. ROMANS 1:20

Ultimately, our ability to perceive and relate to an all-powerful, ever-present, always-loving God is by faith. Faith is the ability to see the unseen, to know that there is more to looks than meets the eye, and it is "by faith we understand that the universe was created by the word of God, so that what is seen was not made out of things that are visible" (Hebrews 11:3). God's Word teaches us to love beyond looks, and the faith he gives empowers us to live it out.

Day Three

How Do You See The Heart of God?

Pray for eyes to see, ears to hear, and a heart to understand God's word today (Deuteronomy 29:4). Then, **write down** John 1:14 or say it out loud:

Talk It Out

1. How do you see the heart of God? Does it change according to your circumstances? Why or why not?

2. In Isaiah 6:3, seraphim are flying around and proclaiming to each other "'Holy, holy, holy is the LORD of hosts; the whole earth is full of his glory!'" R.C. Sproul in his book *The Holiness of God*, says that holiness describes God best:

    Only once is a characteristic of God mentioned three times in succession. The Bible says that God is holy, holy, holy. Not that He is merely holy, or even holy, holy. He is holy, holy, holy. The Bible never says that God is love, love, love; or mercy, mercy, mercy; or wrath, wrath, wrath; or justice, justice, justice. It does say that He is holy, holy, holy, that the whole earth is full of His glory.[5]

Go back and read Isaiah 6: What does Isaiah do in response to the seraphim shouting, "Holy, holy, holy is the LORD of hosts"?

3. Why do you think he says, "For I am a man of unclean lips" instead of "a man with an unclean heart?" See Luke 6:45 for biblical reference.

4. What does God do in response to Isaiah? Look to 1 John 1:9 to see how God responds to us when we confess our sins.

Take It With You

We do not always see God as he is. Jesus steps in to help us by giving us a model to pray: "Pray then like this: 'Our Father in heaven, hallowed be your name'" (Matthew 6:9). As R.C. Sproul says in The Holiness of God, pray for God's name to be hallowed, to be holy not just because it already is, but because you want it to be in your life and on the earth. Take a minute to **pray** the Lord's prayer with the intention of making God's name holy in your life.

How Can You Align Your Heart With God's?

Pray for eyes to see, ears to hear, and a heart to understand God's word today (Deuteronomy 29:4). Then, ***write down*** John 1:14 or say it out loud.

Talk It Out

1. Read Psalm 37:4, which says, "Delight yourself in the Lord, and he will give you the desires of your heart." Focus on the command to "delight yourself in the Lord." Is this command easy or difficult for you? Why or why not?

2. The Bible says our hearts are "deceitful above all things" (Jeremiah 17:9). Ouch. That's a hard truth to hear! But even though our hearts are deceitful, Jesus died to give us new hearts, hearts of flesh, hearts that would desire him, and be delighted in him. What is the current condition of your heart in relation to God?

3. The world tells us to follow our hearts. This can be very dangerous advice if your heart is in the wrong place. The Bible says in Matthew 6:21 that where your treasure is, there your heart will follow. Is your treasure Christ, or the things and desires of this world?

    Jesus enabled us to treasure and desire him when he gave us new hearts (Ezekiel 36:26) and the power of the Holy Spirit (John 14:15-17). John Piper is known for saying, "God is most glorified in us when we are most satisfied in him."[6] When we find joy in the Lord, our affections will follow. When we treasure him, our heart will follow into freedom with Christ. Write down three ways in which God has delighted you today.

    1.

    2.

    3.

Take It With You

Think about the godly people in your life. How do you think they got there? Refer to King David from the Bible. David was certainly not a perfect man, but he was a man after God's own heart (Acts 13:22), and delighted greatly in the Lord. David's desires were for God's desires. **Pray** to be a man or woman after God's own heart.

Group Discussion

Catch up with one another. Drink good drinks, eat good food, or go on a walk together.

1. Pray for God's name to be made holy, for humble hearts, and for honest conversation.
2. Recite John 1:14 out loud to someone or recite it as a group.
3. Review your answers from this past week.
4. Concluding questions:

    a. Has your view of who God is changed since the beginning of this week? How has it changed?
    b. How can you worship God for who he is (see Psalm 51:15-17)?

5. Conclude in prayer. Start by reading 1 John 3:1-2 out loud:

    > See what kind of love the Father has given to us, that we should be called children of God; and so we are. The reason why the world does not know us is that it did not know him. Beloved, we are God's children now, and what we will be has not yet appeared; but we know that when he appears we shall be like him, because we shall see him as he is.

    Give thanks to God for being perfect and loving you perfectly. Ask the Holy Spirit to help you see God for who he says he is.

LEAVING A LEGACY

Day One

Leaving A Legacy For Yourself

You shall love the Lord your God with all your heart and with all your soul and with all your might. And these words that I command you today shall be on your heart. You shall teach them diligently to your children, and shall talk of them when you sit in your house, and when you walk by the way, and when you lie down, and when you rise.

Deuteronomy 6:5-7

Pray for eyes to see, ears to hear, and a heart to understand God's word today (Deuteronomy 29:4). Then, **write down** the memory verse of the week or say it aloud:

Our memory verse for this week, Deuteronomy 6:5-7, asks us to love God with everything we have, teach God's love wherever we are, and remember his love for us and others at all times. One of the best ways to preach the gospel to ourselves is to write down God's work in our lives.

If you have never written down the story of God's grace in your life, this a great time to practice.

Use Romans 12:1 (New International Version) as a reference for how God has used your body for His glory: "Therefore, I urge you, brothers and sisters, in view of God's mercy, to offer your bodies as a living sacrifice, holy and pleasing to God — this is your true and proper worship."

I'll go first and share my story in relation to Romans 12:1:

> I became a Christian in fourth grade. Jesus bought me with a price (1 Corinthians 6:19), and from then on, my body was not my own — I gave it to the Lord. When I was single, I glorified God through playing sports and serving my friends in high school. I continued this as a Young Life leader in college. God taught me happiness through movement and the value of my simple presence in someone else's life. When I got married, I glorified God by sharing my body with my husband.
>
> God taught me, through my husband, that I am completely flawless (Song of Solomon 4:7) because he fully knows me and still fully loves me. The Lord taught me that I can double my joys and halve my sorrows with my husband who loves me as Jesus does. When I got pregnant, I glorified God by birthing new life. God taught me that it's nice to be pretty on the outside, but he created women's bodies to do even more wonderful things than I ever imagined. He taught me the value of children, and the value of being his child — the value of offering myself to him, so I could be a physical part of his miracles.

Talk It Out

What is your story? How have you offered your body as a living sacrifice, and what has God taught you in those seasons? If you haven't given your whole life to the Lord, what's holding you back? Leave a legacy for yourself, and ***write these things down*** as reminders of the work God has done and continues to do in your life.

Take It With You

Be strong and courageous this week and ask someone how they have seen the grace of God in their life. If they aren't sure where to start, be willing to share your story above and begin leaving your legacy.

DAY TWO

Leaving A Legacy For Your Family

Pray for eyes to see, ears to hear, and a heart to understand God's word today (Deuteronomy 29:4). Then, **write down** Deuteronomy 6:5-7 or say it out loud.

We can begin teaching God's love to our children (Deuteronomy 6:5-7) by sharing stories of how we grew up and how our family might have influenced our thoughts and attitudes. You can begin leaving a legacy by loving the family you have now. Let's hear from my friend Emma about how she wants to leave a legacy for her family:

I grew up in a home where dieting was a regular activity, mixed with seasons of eating really poorly. The goal of dieting was always for weight loss and not about being healthy inside and out. The message I took from this mindset was that being healthy was about how I looked, and that my value depended on how I looked.

It has taken me a long time of growing up, repenting of my vanity, and having the Holy Spirit in my heart to understand that the purpose of taking care of my body is not to look a certain way to earn my value in this world. Rather, taking care of myself by exercising and eating well is a way I acknowledge that what God has created is inherently valuable, because it is his creation. And taking care of myself is a way to honor God with my body. I want my children to know that their value is in who they are as a child of God, and not what they look like. They need to know that exercise and eating right are not done to achieve a number on the scale, or to look a certain way, but to steward our physical selves as a gift from God.

Talk It Out

1. How can you leave a legacy for a gospel-centered view of our physical bodies?

2. How can you leave a legacy for your family of valuing others beyond appearances?

3. How can you leave a legacy of loving God for being our Creator? See Joshua 4:21-22 and 1 Samuel 7:12. Do you have an Ebenezer in your house, an object that can testify to God's work in your life? An Ebenezer can be wedding pictures, a framed hymn, a favorite scripture written on a chalkboard, or anything else that represents God's work in your life. You could even use literal stones from Joshua 4 and write what God has done in your life on each of them and put them in an outdoor garden, or just write "Thus far the Lord has helped us" (1 Samuel 7:12 NIV) on one stone, and place it in a visible area of your house.

Take It With You

This week's memory verse says we should teach God's commandments diligently to our children. They are the next generation. They are the future. They can grow up loving God, loving themselves, and loving others. Psalm 78:4 says, "We will not hide them from their children, but tell to the coming generation the glorious deeds of the Lord, and his might, and the wonders that he has done." **Focus** on leaving a legacy in your family right now.

- Eat with them
- Serve them
- Share your testimony

These are some practical ways to start leaving a gospel legacy for your neighbors. *Pray* for them, get to know them and serve them, and share God's grace in your life. ***Write down*** one neighbor you can start praying for today.

Day Four

Leaving a Legacy for Your Community And Beyond

Pray for eyes to see, ears to hear, and a heart to understand God's word today (Deuteronomy 29:4). Then, **write down** Deuteronomy 6:5-7 or say it out loud.

It's difficult to think that one person can leave a legacy for the community and beyond, but then again, Jesus made an impact on the world by investing in twelve people. Jesus' work started before he came to earth, but his life on earth serves as a model for how we can leave a legacy for God's kingdom here and now.

God's people today are a direct result of Jesus' investment in people over 2000 years ago: "It is noteworthy that in the Apostle Paul's writing no less than thirteen times people are called 'fellow worker' (the Greek is synergos). Jesus' legacy is reflected in his life investment in the Twelve."[8]

Talk It Out

1. How can you leave a legacy for a gospel-centered view of our physical bodies in your community and beyond? 2 Peter 1:12-15 specifically addresses this.

2. How can you leave a legacy of valuing others beyond our appearances in your community and beyond? If you need some ideas, start in 1 Peter 3:3-4.

3. How can you leave a legacy of loving God for being our Creator in your community and beyond? Paul speaks about this in Romans 1:8.

Take It With You

If leaving a legacy for your community and beyond sounds overwhelming, start with the first lesson from this week and go from there. Make sure you *know your story* of how you have seen God's grace in your own life before you can share your story with others. Only then can you leave a legacy for your community and leave a mark on the world.

Group Discussion

Catch up with one another. Drink good drinks, eat food food, or go on a walk together.

1. Pray for God's name to be made holy, for humble hearts, and for honest conversation.
2. Recite Deuteronomy 6:5-7 out loud to someone or recite it as a group.
3. Review your answers from this past week's lesson.
4. Concluding questions:

   a. Did you learn anything new about leaving a legacy?
   b. Are you taking any specific action-steps towards leaving a legacy?

5. Conclude in prayer. Start by reading 2 Timothy 4:6-8 out loud:

   For I am already being poured out as a drink offering, and the time of my departure has come. I have fought the good fight, I have finished the race, I have kept the faith. Henceforth there is laid up for me the crown of righteousness, which the Lord, the righteous judge, will award to me on that Day, and not only to me but also to all who have loved his appearing.

Pray that God would give you a vision (Proverbs 29:18) for your legacy, and the desire to advance his kingdom beyond your own life.

Conclusion

I walked into a fine jewelry store the other day to get my wedding ring fixed, when I was struck by the beauty of the diamonds shining in their cases. Why are they so darn beautiful? They're just crystals. They aren't made of light, but they reflect light in so many different ways that you can never get just the right angle to see the whole stone for what it is. It's the same stone but when we look at it, it always seems to be changing and revealing more beauty. I think God's beauty is like that. He talks about a lot of precious jewels in heaven (Revelation 4:2-6) — He is describable, and yet unfathomable in beauty, revealing his form with each reflection of light.

This study is just one facet of God's beauty. You won't be able to fully see God's beauty until heaven, but I'm so grateful you took the time to sit down with scripture and let God reveal his beauty to you and through you. My real hope for you after concluding this study is that you have grown closer to the Lord, and see yourself and others as He sees you. I pray that you are able to identify the lies that the Enemy feeds you about your body and combat them with biblical truth.

My desire is that you will spend more time with Christ that you will glow, just as Moses did when he came down from the mountain (Exodus 34:29). Body image is a lifelong struggle, but I pray that you can walk away with eyes to see, ears to hear, and a heart to understand the Lord and who you are in him.

Notes

[1] "The Dove® Campaign for Real Beauty." The Dove® Campaign for Real Beauty. Accessed August 17, 2015.

[2] Jones, Sally. The Jesus Storybook Bible: Every Story Whispers His Name. Grand Rapids, Mich.: Zonderkidz, 2007.

[3] Keller, Timothy J. The Freedom of Self-forgetfulness: The Path to True Christian Joy. Chorley, England: 10Publishing, 2012.

[4] Tozer, A. W. The Knowledge of the Holy: The Attributes of God, Their Meaning in the Christian Life. New York: Harper & Row, 1961.

[5] Sproul, R. C. The Holiness of God. Wheaton, Ill.: Tyndale House Publishers, 1985.

[6] "We Want You to Be a Christian Hedonist!" Desiring God. August 31, 2006. Accessed August 17, 2015.

[7] "Freedom Of A Christian Martin Luther - Homepage." Lutherans Online. Accessed August 17, 2015.

[8] Mancini, Will, and Tex Dallas. Church Unique: How Missional Leaders Cast Vision, Capture Culture, and Create Movement. San Francisco, CA: Jossey-Bass, 2008.

About The Author

Kasey Shuler lives in Athens, GA, with her husband and daughter. She is a mom, personal fitness trainer, and writer. She is also a fan of Dairy Queen blizzards, a good pun, Speed Scrabble, trampolines, and Nacho Libre. Combined.

Read more at www.kaseybshuler.com.